The Bird of Time

Songs of Life, Death, & the spring

By **Sarojini Naidu**

GYAN

Published by

Gyan Publishing House
5, Ansari Road
Daryaganj, New Delhi-110002
Phone: 011-47034999, 9811692060
E-mail: books@gyanbooks.com

Distribution Network
gyanbooks.com
India, USA, Canada, UK, Australia, France

ISBN: 978-81-212-8256-7 (PB)
First Published, 1912

2nd Impression 2023

Printed at: Gyan Press, Delhi.

THE BIRD OF TIME
Author: SAROJINI NAIDU

The Bird of Time

Sarojini Naidu

The Bird of Time

Songs of Life, Death & the Spring

By Sarojini Naidu

With an Introduction by
Edmund Gosse
And
Portrait of the Author

New York: John Lane Company
London: William Heinemann
1912

DEDICATED

IN TOKEN OF LIFE-LONG HOMAGE AND AFFECTION

TO

MY FATHER

AGHORENATH CHATTOPĀDHYĀY

AND

MY MOTHER

SRIMATI VARADA SUNDARI DEVI

HYDERABAD, DECCAN

May 1912

" The bird of Time has but a little way
To fly . . . and, lo ! the bird is on the wing "

Introduction

IT is only at the request, that is to say at the command, of a dear and valued friend that I consent to write these few sentences. It would seem that an "introduction" can only be needed when the personage to be "introduced" is unknown in a world prepared to welcome her but still ignorant of her qualities. This is certainly not the case with Mrs. Naidu, whose successive volumes, of which this is the third, have been received in Europe with approval, and in India with acclamation. Mrs. Naidu is, I believe, acknowledged to be the most accomplished living poet of India—at least, of those who write in English, since what lyric wonders the native languages of that country may be producing I am not competent to say. But I do not think that any one questions the supreme place she holds among those Indians who choose to write in our tongue. Indeed, I am not disinclined to believe that she is the most brilliant, the most original, as well as the most correct, of all the natives of Hindustan who have written in English. And I say this without prejudice to the fame of that delicious Toru Dutt, so exquisite in her fragility, whose life and poems it was my privilege to reveal to the world thirty years ago. For in the case of Toru Dutt, beautiful as her writings were, there was much in them to be excused by her youth, her solitude, the extremely pathetic circumstances of her brief and melancholy career. In the maturer work of Mrs. Naidu I find nothing, or almost nothing, which the severest criticism could call in question.

In a gracious sentence, published seven or eight years ago, Sarojini Naidu declared that it was the writer of this preface "who first showed" her "the way to the golden threshold" of poetry. This is her generous mode of describing certain conditions which I may perhaps be allowed to enlarge upon so far as they throw light on the contents of the volume before us. It is needless for me to repeat those particulars of the Indian poet's early life, so picturesque and so remarkable, which were given by Mr. Arthur Symons in the excellent essay which he prefixed to her volume of 1905. *Sufficient for my purpose it is to say that when Sarojini Chattopādhyāy—as she then was—first made her appearance in London, she was a child of sixteen years, but as unlike the usual English maiden of that age as a lotus or a cactus is unlike a lily of the valley. She was already marvellous in mental maturity, amazingly well read, and far beyond a Western child in all her acquaintance with the world.*

By some accident—now forgotten, but an accident most fortunate for us—Sarojini was introduced to our house at an early date after her arrival in London, and she soon became one of the most welcome and intimate of our guests. It was natural that one so impetuous and so sympathetic should not long conceal from her hosts the fact that she was writing copiously in verse—in English verse. I entreated to be allowed to see what she had composed, and a bundle of MSS. was slipped into my hand. I hastened to examine it as soon as I was alone, but now there followed a disappointment, and with it an embarrassment, which, in the face of what followed, I make no scruple of revealing. The verses which Sarojini had entrusted to me were skilful in form, correct in grammar and blameless in sentiment, but they had the disadvantage of being totally without individuality. They were Western in feeling and in imagery; they were founded on reminiscences of Tennyson and Shelley; I am not sure that they did not even breathe an atmosphere of Christian resignation. I laid them down in despair; this was but the note of the mocking-bird with a vengeance.

It was not pleasant to daunt the charming and precocious singer by so discouraging a judgment; but I reflected on her youth and her enthusiasm, and I ventured to speak to her sincerely. I advised the consignment of all that she had written, in this falsely English vein, to the waste-paper basket. I implored her to consider that from a young Indian of extreme sensibility, who had mastered not merely the language but the prosody of the West, what we wished to receive was, not a réchauffé of

Anglo-Saxon sentiment in an Anglo-Saxon setting, but some revelation of the heart of India, some sincere penetrating analysis of native passion, of the principles of antique religion and of such mysterious intimations as stirred the soul of the East long before the West had begun to dream that it had a soul. Moreover, I entreated Sarojini to write no more about robins and skylarks, in a landscape of our Midland counties, with the village bells somewhere in the distance calling the parishioners to church, but to describe the flowers, the fruits, the trees, to set her poems firmly among the mountains, the gardens, the temples, to introduce to us the vivid populations of her own voluptuous and unfamiliar province ; in other words, to be a genuine Indian poet of the Deccan, not a clever machine-made imitator of the English classics.

With the docility and the rapid appreciation of genius, Sarojini instantly accepted and with as little delay as possible acted upon this suggestion. Since 1895 she has written, I believe, no copy of verses which endeavours to conceal the exclusively Indian source of her inspiration, and she indulges with too enthusiastic gratitude the friend whose only merit was to show her " the way to the golden threshold." It has been in her earlier collections, and it will be found to be in this, the characteristic of Mrs. Naidu's writing that she is in all things and to the fullest extent autochthonous. She springs from the very soil of India; her spirit, although it employs the English language as its vehicle, has no other tie with the West. It addresses itself to the exposition of emotions which are tropical and primitive, and in this respect, as I believe, if the poems of Sarojini Naidu be carefully and delicately studied they will be found as luminous in lighting up the dark places of the East as any contribution of savant or historian. They have the astonishing advantage of approaching the task of interpretation from inside the magic circle, although armed with a technical skill that has been cultivated with devotion outside of it.

Those who have enjoyed the earlier collections of Mrs. Naidu's poems will find that in " The Bird of Time " the note of girlish ecstasy has passed, and that a graver music has taken its place. She has lived—and this is another facet of her eminent career—in close companionship with sorrow ; she has known the joy and also the despair of consolation. The sight of much suffering, it may be, has thinned her jasmine-garlands and darkened the azure of her sky. It is known to the world that her labours for the public weal have not been carried out without deep injury to her private health. But these things have not slackened the lyric energy of Sarojini ; they have rather given it intensity. She is supported, as the true poet must be, by a noble ambition. In her childhood she dreamed magnificently ; she hopes to be a Goethe or a Keats for India. This desire, like so many others, may prove too heavy a strain for a heart that

> *" s'ouvrit comme une fleur profonde*
> *Dont l'auguste corolle a prédit l'orient."*

But the desire for beauty and fame, the magnificent impulse, are still energetic within this burning soul.

These few words I venture to bring to a close with a couple of sentences from one of her own latest letters: "While I live, it will always be the supreme desire of my Soul to write poetry—one poem, one line of enduring verse even. Perhaps I shall die without realising that longing which is at once an exquisite joy and an unspeakable anguish to me." The reader of "The Bird of Time" will feel satisfied that this her sad apprehension is needless.

EDMUND GOSSE

Contents

Songs of Love and Death

Songs of the Springtime

Indian Folk-Songs

To Indian Tunes

Songs of Life

Songs of Love and Death

A

The Bird of Time

O BIRD of Time on your fruitful bough
What are the songs you sing? . . .
Songs of the glory and gladness of life,
Of poignant sorrow and passionate strife,
And the lilting joy of the spring;
Of hope that sows for the years unborn,
And faith that dreams of a tarrying morn,
The fragrant peace of the twilight's breath,
And the mystic silence that men call death.

O Bird of Time, say where did you learn
The changing measures you sing? . . .
In blowing forests and breaking tides,
In the happy laughter of new-made brides,

And the nests of the new-born spring ;
In the dawn that thrills to a mother's prayer,
And the night that shelters a heart's despair,
In the sigh of pity, the sob of hate,
And the pride of a soul that has conquered fate.

Dirge

In sorrow of her bereavement

WHAT longer need hath she of loveliness
Whom Death has parted from her lord's caress?
Of glimmering robes like rainbow-tangled mist,
Of gleaming glass or jewels on her wrist,
Blossoms or fillet-pearls to deck her head,
Or jasmine garlands to adorn her bed?

Put by the mirror of her bridal days. . . .
Why needs she now its counsel or its praise,
Or happy symbol of the henna leaf
For hands that know the comradeship of grief,
Red spices for her lips that drink of sighs,
Or black collyrium for her weeping eyes?

Shatter her shining bracelets, break the string
Threading the mystic marriage-beads that cling
Loth to desert a sobbing throat so sweet,
Unbind the golden anklets on her feet,
Divest her of her azure veils and cloud
Her living beauty in a living shroud.

. . . . .

Nay, let her be ! . . . what comfort can we give
For joy so frail, for hope so fugitive ?
The yearning pain of unfulfilled delight,
The moonless vigils of her lonely night,
For the abysmal anguish of her tears,
And flowering springs that mock her empty years ?

An Indian Love Song

Written to an Indian tune

He :

Lift up the veils that darken the delicate moon of thy
glory and grace,
Withhold not, O Love, from the night of my longing
the joy of thy luminous face,
Give me a spear of the scented *keora* guarding thy
pinioned curls,
Or a silken thread from the fringes that trouble the
dream of thy glimmering pearls ;
Faint grows my soul with thy tresses' perfume and
the song of thy anklets' caprice,
Revive me, I pray, with the magical nectar that
dwells in the flower of thy kiss.

SHE :

How shall I yield to the voice of thy pleading, how
  shall I grant thy prayer,
Or give thee a rose-red silken tassel, a scented leaf
  from my hair?
Or fling in the flame of thy heart's desire the veils
  that cover my face,
Profane the law of my father's creed for a foe of my
  father's race?
Thy kinsmen have broken our sacred altars and
  slaughtered our sacred kine,
The feud of old faiths and the blood of old battles
  sever thy people and mine.

He:

What are the sins of my race, Beloved, what are my
    people to thee?
And what are thy shrine, and kine and kindred, what
    are thy gods to me?
Love recks not of feuds and bitter follies, of stranger,
    comrade or kin,
Alike in his ear sound the temple bells and the cry of
    the *muezzin*.
For Love shall cancel the ancient wrong and conquer
    the ancient rage,
Redeem with his tears the memoried sorrow that
    sullied a bygone age.

In Remembrance

Violet Clarke—died March 21, 1909

WITH eager knowledge of our ancient lore,
And prescient love of all our ancient race,
You came to us, with gentle hands that bore
Bright gifts of genius, youth, and subtle grace.

Our shrines, our sacred streams, our sumptuous art,
Old hills that scale the sky's unageing dome,
Recalled some long-lost rapture to your heart,
Some far-off memory of your spirit's home.

. . . . .

We said : " She comes, an exquisite, strange flower
From the rich gardens of a northern king ". . .
But lo ! our souls perceived you in that hour
The very rose whereof our poets sing.

Who sped your beauty's seed across the sea,
Bidding you burgeon in that alien clime?
And what prophetic wind of destiny
Restored you to us in your flowering time

For a brief season to delight and bless
Our hearts with delicate splendour and perfume,
Till Death usurped your vivid loveliness
In wanton envy of its radiant bloom?

O frail, miraculous flower, tho' you are dead,
The deathless fragrance of your spirit cleaves
To the dear wreath whereon our tears are shed,
Of your sweet wind-blown and love-garnered Leaves.*

* *"Leaves" is the title of her book of stories, published after her death.*

Love and Death

I DREAMED my love had set thy spirit free,
Enfranchised thee from Fate's o'ermastering power,
And girt thy being with a scatheless dower
Of rich and joyous immortality ;
O Love, I dreamed my soul had ransomed thee,
In thy lone, dread, incalculable hour
From those pale hands at which all mortals cower,
And conquered Death by Love, like Savitri.
When I awoke, alas, my love was vain
E'en to annul one throe of destined pain,
Or by one heart-beat to prolong thy breath ;
O Love, alas, that love could not assuage
The burden of thy human heritage,
Or save thee from the swift decrees of Death.

The Dance of Love

Written for Madame Liza Lehmann

The music sighs and slumbers,
It stirs and sleeps again . . .
Hush, it wakes and weeps and murmurs
Like a woman's heart in pain ;
Now it laughs and calls and coaxes,
Like a lover in the night,
Now it pants with sudden longing,
Now it sobs with spent delight.

Like bright and wind-blown lilies,
The dancers sway and shine,
Swift in a rhythmic circle,
Soft in a rhythmic line ;
Their lithe limbs gleam like amber

Thro' their veils of golden gauze,
As they glide and bend and beckon,
As they wheel and wind and pause.

The voices of lutes and cymbals
Fail on the failing breeze,
And the midnight's soul grows weary
With the scent of the champak trees ;
But the subtle feet of the dancers
In a long, returning chain,
Wake in the heart of lovers
Love's ecstasy and pain.

A Love Song from the North

TELL me no more of thy love, *papeeha*,
Wouldst thou recall to my heart, *papeeha*,
Dreams of delight that are gone,
When swift to my side came the feet of my lover
With stars of the dusk and the dawn?
I see the soft wings of the clouds on the river,
And jewelled with raindrops the mango-leaves quiver,
And tender boughs flower on the plain. . . .
But what is their beauty to me, *papeeha*,
Beauty of blossom and shower, *papeeha*,
That brings not my lover again?

Tell me no more of thy love, *papeeha*,
Wouldst thou revive in my heart, *papeeha*,
Grief for the joy that is gone?

I hear the bright peacock in glimmering woodlands
Cry to its mate in the dawn ;
I hear the black *koel's* slow, tremulous wooing,
And sweet in the gardens the calling and cooing
Of passionate bulbul and dove. . . .
But what is their music to me, *papeeha*,
Songs of their laughter and love, *papeeha*,
To me, forsaken of love ?

The papeeha is a bird that comes in Northern India when the mangoes are ripe, and calls " Pi-kahan, Pi-kahan ? "—Where is my love ?

At Twilight

On the way to Golconda

Weary, I sought kind Death among the rills
That drink of purple twilight where the plain
Broods in the shadow of untroubled hills:
I cried, "High dreams and hope and love are vain,
Absolve my spirit of its poignant ills,
And cleanse me from the bondage of my pain!

"Shall hope prevail where clamorous hate is rife,
Shall sweet love prosper or high dreams find place
Amid the tumult of reverberant strife
'Twixt ancient creeds, 'twixt race and ancient race,
That mars the grave, glad purposes of life,
Leaving no refuge save thy succouring face?"

. . . . .

E'en as I spake, a mournful wind drew near,
Heavy with scent of drooping roses shed,
And incense scattered from the passing bier
Of some loved woman canopied in red,
Borne with slow chant and swift-remembering tear,
To the blind, ultimate silence of the dead. . . .

O lost, O quenched in unawakening sleep
The glory of her dear, reluctant eyes!
O hushed the eager feet that knew the steep
And intricate ways of ecstasy and sighs!
And dumb with alien slumber, dim and deep,
The living heart that was love's paradise!

. . . . .

Quick with the sense of joys she hath foregone,
Returned my soul to beckoning joys that wait,
Laughter of children and the lyric dawn,
And love's delight, profound and passionate,
Winged dreams that blow their golden clarion,
And hope that conquers immemorial hate.

Alone

ALONE, O Love, I seek the blossoming glades,
The bright, accustomed alleys of delight,
Pomegranate-gardens of the mellowing dawn,
Serene and sumptuous orchards of the night.

Alone, O Love, I breast the shimmering waves,
The changing tides of life's familiar streams,
Wide seas of hope, swift rivers of desire,
The moon-enchanted estuary of dreams.

But no compassionate wind or comforting star
Brings me sweet word of thine abiding place . . .
In what predestined hour of joy or tears
Shall I attain the sanctuary of thy face?

A Rajput Love Song

[Parvati *at her lattice*]

O Love! were you a basil-wreath to twine among
my tresses,
A jewelled clasp of shining gold to bind around
my sleeve,
O Love! were you the *keora's* soul that haunts my
silken raiment,
A bright, vermilion tassel in the girdles that I
weave;

O Love! were you the scented fan that lies upon
my pillow,
A sandal lute, or silver lamp that burns before my
shrine,

Why should I fear the jealous dawn that spreads
with cruel laughter,
Sad veils of separation between your face and mine?

Haste, O wild-bee hours to the gardens of the sunset!
Fly, wild-parrot day to the orchards of the west!
Come, O tender night, with your sweet, consoling darkness,
And bring me my Beloved to the shelter of my breast!

[AMAR SINGH *in the saddle*]

O Love! were you the hooded hawk upon my hand
that flutters,
Its collar-band of gleaming bells atinkle as I ride,
O Love! were you a turban-spray or floating heron-
feather,
The radiant, swift, unconquered sword that swingeth
at my side;

O Love! were you a shield against the arrows of my
foemen,
An amulet of jade against the perils of the way,
How should the drum-beats of the dawn divide me
from your bosom,
Or the union of the midnight be ended with the
day?

Haste, O wild-deer hours, to the meadows of the sunset!
Fly, wild stallion day, to the pastures of the west!
Come O tranquil night, with your soft, consenting
darkness,
And bear me to the fragrance of my Beloved's breast!

A Persian Love Song

O Love! I know not why, when you are glad,
Gaily my glad heart leaps.
O Love! I know not why, when you are sad,
Wildly my sad heart weeps.

I know not why, if sweet be your repose,
My waking heart finds rest,
Or if your eyes be dim with pain, sharp throes
Of anguish rend my breast.

Hourly this subtle mystery flowers anew,
O Love, I know not why . . .
Unless it be, perchance, that I am you,
Dear love, that you are I!

To Love

O Love ! of all the riches that are mine,
What gift have I withheld before thy shrine ?

What tender ecstasy of prayer and praise
Or lyric flower of my impassioned days ?

What poignant dream have I denied to thee
Of secret hope, desire and memory ;

Or intimate anguish of sad years, long dead,
Old griefs unstaunched, old fears uncomforted ?

What radiant prophecies that thrill and throng
The unborn years with swift delight of song ?

O Love ! of all the treasures that I own,
What gift have I withheld before thy throne ?

Songs of the Springtime

D

Spring

YOUNG leaves grow green on the banyan twigs,
And red on the peepul tree,
The honey-birds pipe to the budding figs,
And honey-blooms call the bee.

Poppies squander their fragile gold
In the silvery aloe-brake,
Coral and ivory lilies unfold
Their delicate lives on the lake.

Kingfishers ruffle the feathery sedge,
And all the vivid air thrills
With butterfly-wings in the wild-rose hedge,
And the luminous blue of the hills.

Kamala tinkles a lingering foot
In the grove where temple-bells ring,
And Krishna plays on his bamboo flute
An idyl of love and spring.

A Song in Spring

WILD bees that rifle the mango blossom,
Set free awhile from the love-god's string,
Wild birds that sway in the citron branches,
Drunk with the rich, red honey of spring,

Fireflies weaving aërial dances
In fragile rhythms of flickering gold,
What do you know in your blithe, brief season
Of dreams deferred and a heart grown old?

But the wise winds know, as they pause to slacken
The speed of their subtle, omniscient flight,
Divining the magic of unblown lilies,
Foretelling the stars of the unborn night.

They have followed the hurrying feet of pilgrims,
Tracking swift prayers to their utmost goals,
They have spied on Love's old and changeless secret,
And the changing sorrow of human souls.

They have tarried with Death in her parleying-places,
And issued the word of her high decree,
Their wings have winnowed the garnered sunlight,
Their lips have tasted the purple sea.

The Joy of the Springtime

SPRINGTIME, O Springtime, what is your essence,
The lilt of a bulbul, the laugh of a rose,
The dance of the dew on the wings of a moonbeam,
The voice of the zephyr that sings as he goes,
The hope of a bride or the dream of a maiden
Watching the petals of gladness unclose?

Springtime, O Springtime, what is your secret,
The bliss at the core of your magical mirth,
That quickens the pulse of the morning to wonder
And hastens the seeds of all beauty to birth,
That captures the heavens and conquers to blossom
The roots of delight in the heart of the earth?

Vasant Panchami

Lilavati's Lament at the Feast of Spring

Go, dragon-fly, fold up your purple wing,
Why will you bring me tidings of the spring?
O lilting *koels*, hush your rapturous notes,
O *dhadikulas*, still your passionate throats,
Or seek some further garden for your nest . . .
Your songs are poisoned arrows in my breast.

O quench your flame, ye crimson *gulmohors*,
That flaunt your dazzling bloom across my doors,
Furl your white bells, sweet *champa* buds that call
Wild bees to your ambrosial festival,
And hold your breath, O dear *sirisha* trees . . .
You slay my heart with bitter memories.

O joyous girls who rise at break of morn
With sandal-soil your thresholds to adorn,
Ye brides who streamward bear on jewelled feet
Your gifts of silver lamps and new-blown wheat,
I pray you dim your voices when you sing
Your radiant salutations to the spring.

Hai! what have I to do with nesting birds,
With lotus-honey, corn and ivory curds,
With plantain blossom and pomegranate fruit,
Or rose-wreathed lintels and rose-scented lute,
With lighted shrines and fragrant altar-fires
Where happy women breathe their hearts' desires?

For my sad life is doomed to be, alas,
Ruined and sere like sorrow-trodden grass,
My heart hath grown, plucked by the wind of grief,
Akin to fallen flower and faded leaf,

Akin to every lone and withered thing
That hath foregone the kisses of the spring.

The Vasant Panchami is the spring festival when Hindu girls and married women carry gifts of lighted lamps and new-grown corn as offerings to the goddess of the spring and set them afloat on the face of the waters. Hindu widows cannot take part in any festive ceremonials. Their portion is sorrow and austerity.

In a Time of Flowers

O Love ! do you know the spring is here
With the lure of her magic flute ? . . .
The old earth breaks into passionate bloom
At the kiss of her fleet, gay foot.
The burgeoning leaves on the almond boughs,
And the leaves on the blue wave's breast
Are crowned with the limpid and delicate light
Of the gems in your turban-crest.
The bright pomegranate buds unfold,
The frail wild lilies appear,
Like the blood-red jewels you used to fling
O'er the maidens that danced at the feast of spring
To welcome the new-born year.

O Love! do you know the spring is here? . . .
The dawn and the dusk grow rife
With scent and song and tremulous mirth,
The blind, rich travail of life.
The winds are drunk with the odorous breath
Of *henna*, *sarisha*, and *neem* . . .
Do they ruffle your cold, strange, tranquil sleep,
Or trouble your changeless dream
With poignant thoughts of the world you loved,
And the beauty you held so dear?
Do you long for a brief, glad hour to wake
From your lonely slumber for sweet love's sake,
To welcome the new-born year?

In Praise of Gulmohur Blossoms

WHAT can rival your lovely hue
O gorgeous boon of the spring?
The glimmering red of a bridal robe,
Rich red of a wild bird's wing?
Or the mystic blaze of the gem that burns
On the brow of a serpent-king?

What can rival the valiant joy
Of your dazzling, fugitive sheen?
The limpid clouds of the lustrous dawn
That colour the ocean's mien?
Or the blood that poured from a thousand breasts
To succour a Rajput queen? *

* *Queen Padmini of Chitore, famous in Indian history and song.*

What can rival the radiant pride
Of your frail, victorious fire?
The flame of hope or the flame of hate,
Quick flame of my heart's desire?
Or the rapturous light that leaps to heaven
From a true wife's funeral pyre?

Nasturtiums

POIGNANT and subtle and bitter perfume,
Exquisite, luminous, passionate bloom,
Your leaves interwoven of fragrance and fire
Are Savitri's sorrow and Sita's desire,
Draupadi's longing, Damayanti's fears,
And sweetest Sakuntala's magical tears.

These are the immortal women of Sanscrit legend and song, whose poignant sorrows and radiant virtues still break the heart and inspire the lives of Indian women.

Golden Cassia

O BRILLIANT blossoms that strew my way,
You are only woodland flowers they say.

But, I sometimes think that perchance you are
Fragments of some new-fallen star ;

Or golden lamps for a fairy shrine,
Or golden pitchers for fairy wine.

Perchance you are, O frail and sweet !
Bright anklet-bells from the wild spring's feet,

Or the gleaming tears that some fair bride shed
Remembering her lost maidenhead.

But now, in the memoried dusk you seem
The glimmering ghosts of a bygone dream.

Champak Blossoms

Amber petals, ivory petals,
Petals of carven jade,
Charming with your ambrosial sweetness
Forest and field and glade,
Foredoomed in your hour of transient glory
To shrivel and shrink and fade !

Tho' mango blossoms have long since vanished,
And orange blossoms be shed,
They live anew in the luscious harvests
Of ripening yellow and red ;
But you, when your delicate bloom is over,
Will reckon amongst the dead.

Only to girdle a girl's dark tresses
Your fragrant hearts are uncurled :
Only to garland the vernal breezes
Your fragile stars are unfurled.
You make no boast in your purposeless beauty
To serve or profit the world.

Yet, 'tis of you thro' the moonlit ages
That maidens and minstrels sing,
And lay your buds on the great god's altar,
O radiant blossoms that fling
Your rich, voluptuous, magical perfume
To ravish the winds of spring.

Ecstasy

HEART, O my heart! lo, the springtime is waking
In meadow and grove.
Lo, the mellifluous *koels* are making
Their pæans of love.
Behold the bright rivers and rills in their glancing,
Melodious flight,
Behold how the sumptuous peacocks are dancing
In rhythmic delight.

Shall we in the midst of life's exquisite chorus
Remember our grief,
O heart, when the rapturous season is o'er us
Of blossom and leaf?

Their joy from the birds and the streams let us borrow,
O heart ! let us sing,
The years are before us for weeping and sorrow . . .
To-day it is spring !

Indian Folk-Songs

To Indian Tunes

Village Song

Full are my pitchers and far to carry,
Lone is the way and long,
Why, O why was I tempted to tarry
Lured by the boatmen's song?
Swiftly the shadows of night are falling,
Hear, O hear, is the white crane calling,
Is it the wild owl's cry?
There are no tender moonbeams to light me,
If in the darkness a serpent should bite me,
Or if an evil spirit should smite me,
Rām re Rām! I shall die.

My brother will murmur "Why doth she linger?"
My mother will wait and weep,
Saying, "O safe may the great gods bring her,
The Jamuna's waters are deep." . . .

The Jamuna's waters rush by so quickly,
The shadows of evening gather so thickly,
Like black birds in the sky. . . .
O ! if the storm breaks, what will betide me ?
Safe from the lightning where shall I hide me ?
Unless Thou succour my footsteps and guide me,
Rām re Rām ! I shall die.

Slumber Song for Sunalini

In a Bengalee metre

WHERE the golden, glowing
Champak-buds are blowing,
By the swiftly-flowing streams,
Now, when day is dying,
There are fairies flying
Scattering a cloud of dreams.

Slumber-spirits winging
Thro' the forest singing,
Flutter hither bringing soon,
Baby-visions sheeny
For my Sunalini . . .
Hush thee, O my pretty moon !

Sweet, the saints shall bless thee . . .
Hush, mine arms caress thee,

Hush, my heart doth press thee, sleep,
Till the red dawn dances
Breaking thy soft trances,
Sleep, my Sunalini, sleep !

Songs of my City

I. In a Latticed Balcony

How shall I feed thee, Beloved?
On golden-red honey and fruit.
How shall I please thee, Beloved?
With th' voice of the cymbal and lute.

How shall I garland thy tresses?
With pearls from the jessamine close.
How shall I perfume thy fingers?
With th' soul of the keora and rose.

How shall I deck thee, O Dearest?
In hues of the peacock and dove.
How shall I woo thee, O Dearest?
With the delicate silence of love.

II. In the Bazaars of Hyderabad

To a tune of the Bazaars

WHAT do you sell, O ye merchants?
Richly your wares are displayed.
Turbans of crimson and silver,
Tunics of purple brocade,
Mirrors with panels of amber,
Daggers with handles of jade.

What do you weigh, O ye vendors?
Saffron and lentil and rice.
What do you grind, O ye maidens?
Sandalwood, henna, and spice.
What do you call, O ye pedlars?
Chessmen and ivory dice.

What do you make, O ye goldsmiths?
Wristlet and anklet and ring,

Bells for the feet of blue pigeons,
Frail as a dragon-fly's wing,
Girdles of gold for the dancers,
Scabbards of gold for the king.

What do you cry, O ye fruitmen?
Citron, pomegranate, and plum.
What do you play, O musicians?
Cithār, sarangi, and drum.
What do you chant, O magicians?
Spells for the æons to come.

What do you weave, O ye flower-girls
With tassels of azure and red?
Crowns for the brow of a bridegroom,
Chăplets to garland his bed,
Sheets of white blossoms new-gathered
To perfume the sleep of the dead.

Bangle-sellers

BANGLE-SELLERS are we who bear
Our shining loads to the temple fair. . . .
Who will buy these delicate, bright
Rainbow-tinted circles of light?
Lustrous tokens of radiant lives,
For happy daughters and happy wives.

Some are meet for a maiden's wrist,
Silver and blue as the mountain-mist,
Some are flushed like the buds that dream
On the tranquil brow of a woodland stream;
Some are aglow with the bloom that cleaves
To the limpid glory of new-born leaves.

Some are like fields of sunlit corn,
Meet for a bride on her bridal morn,
Some, like the flame of her marriage fire,
Or rich with the hue of her heart's desire,
Tinkling, luminous, tender, and clear,
Like her bridal laughter and bridal tear.

Some are purple and gold-flecked grey,
For her who has journeyed thro' life midway,
Whose hands have cherished, whose love has blest
And cradled fair sons on her faithful breast,
Who serves her household in fruitful pride,
And worships the gods at her husband's side.

The Festival of Serpents

SHINING ones awake, we seek your chosen temples
In caves and sheltering sandhills and sacred banyan
roots ;
O lift your dreaming heads from their trance of age-
less wisdom,
And weave your mystic measures to the melody of
flutes.

We bring you milk and maize, wild figs and golden
honey,
And kindle fragrant incense to hallow all the air,
With fasting lips we pray, with fervent hearts we
praise you,
O bless our lowly offerings and hearken to our
prayer.

Guard our helpless lives and guide our patient
labours,
And cherish our dear vision like the jewels in your
crests ;
O spread your hooded watch for the safety of our
slumbers,
And soothe the troubled longings that clamour in
our breasts.

Swift are ye as streams and soundless as the dewfall,
Subtle as the lightning and splendid as the sun ;
Seers are ye and symbols of the ancient silence,
Where life and death and sorrow and ecstasy are
one.

Song of Radha the Milkmaid

I CARRIED my curds to the Mathura fair. . . .
How softly the heifers were lowing. . . .
I wanted to cry "Who will buy, who will buy
These curds that are white as the clouds in the sky
When the breezes of *Shrawan* are blowing?"
But my heart was so full of your beauty, Beloved,
They laughed as I cried without knowing:
Govinda! Govinda!
Govinda! Govinda! . . .
How softly the river was flowing!

I carried my pots to the Mathura tide. . . .
How gaily the rowers were rowing! . . .
My comrades called "Ho! let us dance, let us sing
And wear saffron garments to welcome the spring,

And pluck the new buds that are blowing."
But my heart was so full of your music, Beloved,
They mocked when I cried without knowing :

Govinda ! Govinda !
Govinda ! Govinda ! . . .

How gaily the river was flowing !

I carried my gifts to the Mathura shrine. . . .
How brightly the torches were glowing ! . . .
I folded my hands at the altars to pray
" O shining Ones guard us by night and by day "—
And loudly the conch shells were blowing.
But my heart was so lost in your worship, Beloved,
They were wroth when I cried without knowing :

Govinda ! Govinda !
Govinda ! Govinda ! . . .

How brightly the river was flowing !

Mathura is the chief centre of the mystic worship of Khrishna, the Divine Cowherd and Musician—the "Divine Beloved" of every Hindu heart. He is also called Govinda.

Spinning Song

PAMDINI:

MY sisters plucked green leaves at morn
To deck the garden swing,
And donned their shining golden veils
For the Festival of Spring. . . .
But sweeter than the new-blown vines,
And the call of nesting birds
Are the tendrils of your hair, Beloved,
And the music of your words.

MAYURA:

My sisters sat beside the hearth
Kneading the saffron cakes,
They gathered honey from the hives
For the Festival of Snakes. . . .

Why should I wake the jewelled lords
With offerings or vows,
Who wear the glory of your love
Like a jewel on my brows?

SARASVATI:
My sisters sang at evenfall
A hymn of ancient rites,
And kindled rows of silver lamps
For the Festival of Lights. . . .
But I leaned against the lattice-door
To watch the kindling skies,
And praised the gracious gods, Beloved,
For the beauty of your eyes.

The Festivals are known respectively as the Vasant Panchami, Nagpanchami, and Depavali.

Hymn to Indra, Lord of Rain

Men's Voices:

O Thou, who rousest the voice of the thunder,
And biddest the storms to awake from their sleep,
Who breakest the strength of the mountains asunder,
And cleavest the manifold pride of the deep!
Thou, who with bountiful torrent and river
Dost nourish the heart of the forest and plain,
Withhold not Thy gifts O Omnipotent Giver!
Hearken, O Lord of Rain!

Women's Voices:

O Thou, who wieldest Thy deathless dominion
O'er mutable legions of earth and the sky,
Who grantest the eagle the joy of her pinion,
And teachest the young of the *koel* to fly!

Thou who art mighty to succour and cherish,
Who savest from sorrow and shieldest from pain,
Withhold not Thy merciful love, or we perish,
Hearken, O Lord of Rain !

Songs of Life

Death and Life

DEATH stroked my hair and whispered tenderly :
" Poor child, shall I redeem thee from thy pain,
Renew thy joy and issue thee again
Inclosed in some renascent ecstasy . . .
Some lilting bird or lotus-loving bee,
Or the diaphanous silver of the rain,
Th' alluring scent of the sirisha-plain,
The wild wind's voice, the white wave's melody ? "

I said, " Thy gentle pity shames mine ear,
O Death, am I so purposeless a thing,
Shall my soul falter or my body fear
Its poignant hour of bitter suffering,
Or fail ere I achieve my destined deed
Of song or service for my country's need ? "

The Hussain Saagar

THE young dawn woos thee with his amorous grace,
The journeying clouds of sunset pause and hover,
Drinking the beauty of thy luminous face,
But none thine inmost glory may discover,
For thine evasive silver doth enclose
What secret purple and what subtle rose
Responsive only to the wind, thy lover.
Only for him thy shining waves unfold
Translucent music answering his control ;
Thou dost, like me, to one allegiance hold,
O lake, O living image of my soul.

The Faery Isle of Janjira

To Her Highness Nazli Raffia, Begum of Janjira

FAIN would I dwell in your faery kingdom,
O faery queen of a flowering clime,
Where life glides by to a delicate measure,
With the glamour and grace of a far-off time.

Fain would I dwell where your wild doves wander,
Your palm-woods burgeon and sea-winds sing. . . .
Lulled by the rune of the rhythmic waters,
In your Island of Bliss it is always spring.

Yet must I go where the loud world beckons,
And the urgent drum-beat of destiny calls,
Far from your white dome's luminous slumber,
Far from the dream of your fortress walls,

Into the strife of the throng and the tumult,
The war of sweet Love against folly and wrong ;
Where brave hearts carry the sword of battle,
'Tis mine to carry the banner of song,

The solace of faith to the lips that falter,
The succour of hope to the hands that fail,
The tidings of joy when Peace shall triumph,
When Truth shall conquer and Love prevail.

The Soul's Prayer

In childhood's pride I said to Thee:
"O Thou, who mad'st me of Thy breath,
Speak, Master, and reveal to me
Thine inmost laws of life and death.

"Give me to drink each joy and pain
Which Thine eternal hand can mete,
For my insatiate soul would drain
Earth's utmost bitter, utmost sweet.

"Spare me no bliss, no pang of strife,
Withhold no gift or grief I crave,
The intricate lore of love and life
And mystic knowledge of the grave."

Lord, Thou didst answer stern and low:
"Child, I will hearken to thy prayer,
And thy unconquered soul shall know
All passionate rapture and despair.

"Thou shalt drink deep of joy and fame,
And love shall burn thee like a fire,
And pain shall cleanse thee like a flame,
To purge the dross from thy desire.

"So shall thy chastened spirit yearn
To seek from its blind prayer release,
And spent and pardoned, sue to learn
The simple secret of My peace.

"I, bending from my sevenfold height
Will teach thee of My quickening grace,
Life is a prism of My light,
And Death the shadow of My face."

Transience

NAY, do not grieve tho' life be full of sadness,
Dawn will not veil her splendour for your grief,
Nor spring deny their bright, appointed beauty
To lotus blossom and ashoka leaf.

Nay, do not pine, tho' life be dark with trouble,
Time will not pause or tarry on his way ;
To-day that seems so long, so strange, so bitter,
Will soon be some forgotten yesterday.

Nay, do not weep ; new hopes, new dreams, new faces,
The unspent joy of all the unborn years,
Will prove your heart a traitor to its sorrow,
And make your eyes unfaithful to their tears.

The Old Woman

A LONELY old woman sits out in the street
'Neath the boughs of a banyan tree,
And hears the bright echo of hurrying feet,
The pageant of life going blithely and fleet
    To the feast of eternity.

Her tremulous hand holds a battered white bowl,
If perchance in your pity you fling her a dole ;
She is poor, she is bent, she is blind,
But she lifts a brave heart to the jest of the days,
And her withered, brave voice croons its pæan of
    praise,
Be the gay world kind or unkind :
  "*La ilaha illa-l-Allah,*
  La ilaha illa-l-Allah,
  Muhammad-ar-Rasul-Allah."

In hope of your succour, how often in vain,
So patient she sits at my gates,
In the face of the sun and the wind and the rain,
Holding converse with poverty, hunger and pain,
And the ultimate sleep that awaits. . . .
In her youth she hath comforted lover and son,
In her weary old age, O dear God, is there none
To bless her tired eyelids to rest? . . .
Tho' the world may not tarry to help her or heed,
More clear than the cry of her sorrow and need
Is the faith that doth solace her breast:
"*La ilaha illa-l-Allah,*
La ilaha illa-l-Allah,
Muhammad-ar-Rasul-Allah."

In the Night

SLEEP, O my little ones, sleep,
Safe till the daylight be breaking . . .
We have long vigils to keep,
Harvests to sow while you sleep,
Fair for the hour of your waking,
Ripe for your sickles to reap.

Sleep, O my little ones, sleep,
Yours is the golden To-morrow,
Yours are the hands that will reap
Dreams that we sow while you sleep,
Fed with our hope and our sorrow,
Rich with the tears that we weep.

At Dawn

CHILDREN, my children, the daylight is breaking,
The cymbals of morn sound the hour of your waking,
The long night is o'er, and our labour is ended,
Fair blow the fields that we tilled and we tended,
Swiftly the harvest grows mellow for reaping,
The harvest we sowed in the time of your sleeping.

Weak were our hands but our service was tender,
In darkness we dreamed of the dawn of your splendour,
In silence we strove for the joy of the morrow,
And watered your seeds from the wells of our sorrow,
We toiled to enrich the glad hour of your waking,
Our vigil is done, lo ! the daylight is breaking.

Children, my children, who wake to inherit
The ultimate hope of our travailing spirit,
Say, when your young hearts shall take to their
keeping
The manifold dreams we have sown for your reaping,
Is it praise, is it pain you will grant us for guerdon ?
Anoint with your love or arraign with your pardon ?

An Anthem of Love

Two hands are we to serve thee, O our Mother,
To strive and succour, cherish and unite;
Two feet are we to cleave the waning darkness,
And gain the pathways of the dawning light.

Two ears are we to catch the nearing echo,
The sounding cheer of Time's prophetic horn;
Two eyes are we to reap the crescent glory,
The radiant promise of renascent morn.

One heart are we to love thee, O our Mother,
One undivided, indivisible soul,
Bound by one hope, one purpose, one devotion
Towards a great, divinely-destined goal.

Solitude

LET us rise, O my heart, let us go where the twilight is calling
Far away from the sound of this lonely and menacing crowd,
To the glens, to the glades, where the magical darkness is falling
In rivers of gold from the breast of a radiant cloud.

Come away, come away from this throng and its tumult of sorrow,
There is rest, there is peace from the pang of its manifold strife
Where the halcyon night holds in trust the dear songs of the morrow,
And the silence is but a rich pause in the music of life.

Let us climb where the eagles keep guard on the
rocky grey ledges,
Let us lie 'neath the palms where perchance we may
listen, and reach
A delicate dream from the lips of the slumbering
sedges,
That catch from the stars some high tone of their
mystical speech.

Or perchance, we may glean a far glimpse of the
Infinite Bosom
In whose glorious shadow all life is unfolded or
furled,
Thro' the luminous hours ere the lotus of dawn shall
reblossom
In petals of splendour to worship the Lord of the
world.

A Challenge to Fate

Why will you vex me with your futile conflict,
Why will you strive with me, O foolish Fate?
You cannot break me with your poignant envy,
You cannot slay me with your subtle hate:
For all the cruel folly you pursue
I will not cry with suppliant hands to you.

You may perchance wreck in your bitter malice
The radiant empire of mine eager eyes . . .
Say, can you rob my memory's dear dominion
O'er sunlit mountains and sidereal skies?
In my enduring treasuries I hold
Their ageless splendour of unravished gold.

You may usurp the kingdoms of my hearing . . .
Say, shall my scatheless spirit cease to hear

The bridal rapture of the blowing valleys,
The lyric pageant of the passing year,
The sounding odes and surging harmonies
Of battling tempests and unconquered seas?

Yea, you may smite my mouth to throbbing
silence,
Pluck from my lips power of articulate words . . .
Say, shall my heart lack its familiar language
While earth has nests for her mellifluous birds?
Shall my impassioned heart forget to sing
With the ten thousand voices of the spring?

Yea, you may quell my blood with sudden anguish,
Fetter my limbs with some compelling pain . . .
How will you daunt my free, far-journeying fancy
That rides upon the pinions of the rain?
How will you tether my triumphant mind,
Rival and fearless comrade of the wind?

. . . . .

Tho' you deny the hope of all my being,
Betray my love, my sweetest dream destroy,
Yet will I slake my individual sorrow
At the deep source of Universal joy. . . .
O Fate, in vain you hanker to control
My frail, serene, indomitable soul.

The Call to Evening Prayer

Allah ho Akbar ! Allah ho Akbar !
From mosque and minar the muezzins are calling ;
Pour forth your praises, O Chosen of Islam ;
Swiftly the shadows of sunset are falling :
Allah ho Akbar ! Allah ho Akbar !

Avė Maria ! Ave Maria !
Devoutly the priests at the altars are singing ;
O ye who worship the Son of the Virgin,
Make your orisons, the vespers are ringing :
Ave Maria ! Ave Maria !

Ahura Mazda ! Ahura Mazda !
How the sonorous Avesta is flowing !

Ye, who to Flame and the light make obeisance,
Bend low where the quenchless blue torches are
glowing :

Ahura Mazda ! Ahura Mazda !
Naray'yana ! Naray'yana !
Hark to the ageless, divine invocation !
Lift up your hands, O ye children of Bramha,
Lift up your voices in rapt adoration :
Naray'yana ! Naray'yana !

In Salutation to the Eternal Peace

MEN say the world is full of fear and hate,
And all life's ripening harvest-fields await
The restless sickle of relentless fate.

But I, sweet Soul, rejoice that I was born,
When from the climbing terraces of corn
I watch the golden orioles of Thy morn.

What care I for the world's desire and pride,
Who know the silver wings that gleam and glide,
The homing pigeons of Thine eventide?

What care I for the world's loud weariness,
Who dream in twilight granaries Thou dost bless
With delicate sheaves of mellow silences?

Say, shall I heed dull presages of doom,
Or dread the rumoured loneliness and gloom,
The mute and mythic terror of the tomb ?

For my glad heart is drunk and drenched with Thee,
O inmost wine of living ecstasy !
O intimate essence of eternity !

Medley

A Kashmeri Song

THE poppy grows on the roof-top,
The iris flowers on the grave;
Hope in the heart of a lover,
And fear in the heart of a slave.

The opal lies in the river,
The pearl in the ocean's breast;
Doubt in a grieving bosom,
And faith in a heart at rest.

Fireflies dance in the moon-light,
Peach-leaves dance in the wind;
Dreams and delicate fancies
Dance thro' a poet's mind.

Sweetness dwells in the beehive,
And lives in a maiden's breath ;
Joy in the eyes of children
And peace in the hands of Death.

Farewell

Bright shower of lambent butterflies,
Soft cloud of murmuring bees,
O fragile storm of sighing leaves
Adrift upon the breeze !

Wild birds with eager wings outspread
To seek an alien sky,
Sweet comrades of a lyric spring.
My little songs, good-bye !

Guerdon

To field and forest
The gifts of the spring,
To hawk and to heron
The pride of their wing ;
Her grace to the panther,
Her tints to the dove. . . .
For me, O my Master,
The rapture of Love !

To the hand of the diver
The gems of the tide,
To the eyes of the bridegroom
The face of his bride ;

To the heart of a dreamer
The dreams of his youth. . . .
For me, O my Master,
The rapture of Truth !

To priests and to prophets
The joy of their creeds,
To kings and their cohorts
The glory of deeds ;
And peace to the vanquished
And hope to the strong. . . .
For me, O my Master,
The rapture of Song !